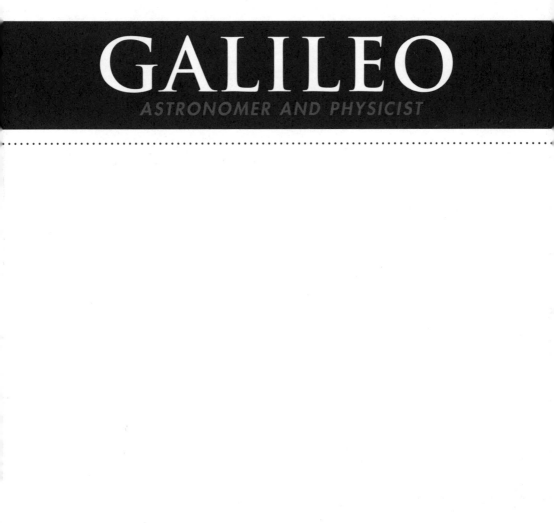

# GALILEO
## ASTRONOMER AND PHYSICIST

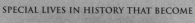

SPECIAL LIVES IN HISTORY THAT BECOME

*Signature* LIVES

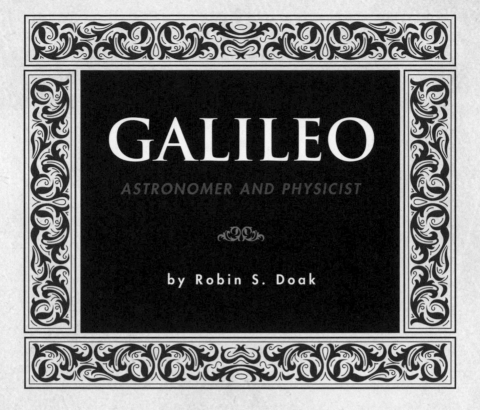

# GALILEO

## ASTRONOMER AND PHYSICIST

by Robin S. Doak

Content Adviser: Kerry Magruder, Ph.D.,
Librarian and Adjunct Professor,
History of Science Department, University of Oklahoma

Reading Adviser: Rosemary G. Palmer, Ph.D.,
Department of Literacy, College of Education,
Boise State University

COMPASS POINT BOOKS ✦ MINNEAPOLIS, MINNESOTA

Compass Point Books
3109 West 50th Street, #115
Minneapolis, MN 5541

Visit Compass Point Books on the Internet at *www.compasspointbooks.com*
or e-mail your request to *custserv@compasspointbooks.com.*

Editor: Jennifer VanVoorst
Lead Designer: Jaime Martens
Photo Researcher: Svetlana Zhurkina
Page Production: Heather Griffin
Cartographer: XNR Productions, Inc.
Educational Consultant: Diane Smolinski

Managing Editor: Catherine Neitge
Art Director: Keith Griffin
Production Director: Keith McCormick
Creative Director: Terri Foley

**Library of Congress Cataloging-in-Publication Data**
Doak, Robin S. (Robin Santos), 1963–
 Galileo : astronomer and physicist / by Robin S. Doak.
   p. cm. — (Signature lives)
 Includes bibliographical references and index.
 ISBN-13: 978-0-7565-0813-5 (hardcover)
 ISBN-10: 0-7565-0813-4 (hardcover)
 ISBN-13: 978-0-7565-1059-6 (paperback)
 ISBN-10: 0-7565-1059-7 (paperback)
 1. Galilei, Galileo, 1564–1642—Juvenile literature. 2. Astronomers—
Italy—Biography—Juvenile literature. 3. Physicists—Italy—
Biography—Juvenile literature. I. Title. II. Series.
 QB36.G2D65 2005
 520'.092—dc22i                          2004019031

*Signature Lives*

# RENAISSANCE ERA

The Renaissance was a cultural movement that started in Italy in the early 1300s. The word *renaissance* comes from a Latin word meaning "rebirth," and during this time, Europe experienced a rebirth of interest and achievement in the arts, science, and global exploration. People reacted against the religion-centered culture of the Middle Ages to find greater value in the human world. By the time the Renaissance came to a close, around 1600, people had come to look at their world in a brand new way.

Galileo

# Table of Contents

# 1 THE FATHER OF MODERN SCIENCE

A murmur went through the Vatican courtroom as the elderly man was led to the dock. Could it be, people wondered, that this small, unassuming scientist named Galileo Galilei was the one who had caused so much trouble for the Catholic Church? The man faced down questions one by one, explaining his beliefs and professing his innocence. By supporting the view of the universe held by Polish astronomer Nicolaus Copernicus against the long-held teachings of the church, Galileo had angered church leaders and became a target of the Inquisition. He was on trial for heresy.

Four centuries ago, in Galileo's time, the church taught that all the stars and planets revolved around Earth. Copernicus and Galileo, however, believed

*In 1633, Galileo Galilei stood trial before the Roman Catholic Inquisition for supporting the view of a sun-centered solar system.*

*Copernicus's theories of a solar system in which Earth revolves around the sun went against the teachings of the Catholic Church.*

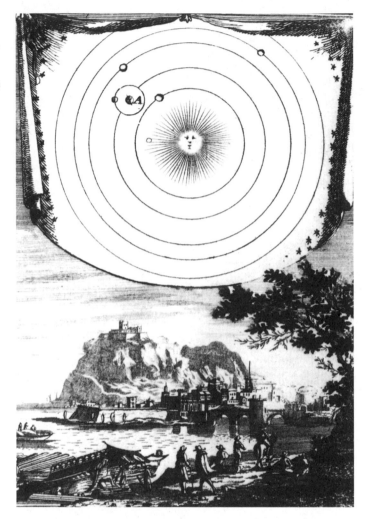

that Earth actually revolved around the sun. Using the new telescope he had made, Galileo showed that Copernicus's theories were true. But ultimately Galileo's claims of innocence would not be enough to set him free. He would become known as a martyr for truth and the father of modern science.

In today's world, people take many facts about the world around them for granted. For instance, people today know that the sun is the center of our solar system and that Earth revolves around it. People understand gravity, motion, and many other aspects of science.

Four centuries ago, however, people did not know these basic facts. Science, the study of the universe through observing, experimenting, and testing, was then in its early stages. People relied instead on the explanations developed by ancient Greek philosophers hundreds of years earlier.

In the late 1500s, one man in Italy stepped forward to revolutionize science and forever change the way people looked at their world. Galileo was an astronomer, physicist, mathematician, writer, and inventor. He created or refined many useful devices that are still in use today. Galileo helped to develop the scientific method, a system of proving a theory through careful testing and a process that forms the

*Galileo lived at a time when very famous and well-respected Italians were honored by being called only by their first names. Before Galileo, there were the artists Michelangelo (Buonarroti) and Leonardo (da Vinci) and the poet Dante (Alighieri). Throughout his life, Galileo Galilei was known by his first name. When writing books and letters, the scientist often signed only the name "Galileo." All of his friends, admirers, and opponents also knew him by that name.*

backbone of modern science. Albert Einstein, another great scientist, called Galileo "the father of modern physics—indeed of modern science altogether." And yet, it is not Galileo's scientific advances alone that have made him famous. His struggle against the philosophers, clergy, and other scientists of his day has made him both a legend of science and a popular hero.

Galileo lived during an age when the Roman Catholic Church was still the most powerful institution in Italy. But with the beginning of the Renaissance, a historic period that stretched from the 14th to the 16th century, things changed. During this time, people became interested in art, exploration, and knowledge. They began to exercise their individual powers outside of the group.

*One important Renaissance innovation was the printing press, which allowed books to be "mass produced." Before its invention in 1454, books could take months—even years—to create, because each copy had to be written out by hand. The printing press allowed new information, ideas, and discoveries to spread to greater numbers of people.*

Although Rome and the popes had earlier embraced the creative spirit of the Renaissance, times were changing again. In the 1500s, a religious revolution swept across Europe. People who wanted to reform the Catholic Church had become more outspoken. In 1517, German priest Martin Luther wrote a document called the

*Catholic priest Martin Luther started the Protestant Reformation when he challenged practices of the church.*

*Ninety-Five Theses* that attacked some of the church's practices. Roman Catholic officials were furious, and Luther was excommunicated, or removed from the Catholic Church. Luther and his followers became known as "Protestants," because they

*In Galileo's time, the Catholic Church was the most powerful institution in Italy.*

protested against the Catholic Church.

The Protestant Reformation caused Catholic officials to fear people with new ideas, especially those that threatened the church itself. As a result, church officials in the late 1500s became less willing to entertain new thoughts and theories about science and philosophy.

During this time, the Catholic Church tried to keep control over the minds and hearts of its followers. Catholic leaders did not want people questioning their authority. They were especially concerned with people who were beginning to question the words of the Bible or interpreting the Bible without help from their priests. In 1546, the church passed a decree stating that "no one relying on his own judgment...shall dare to interpret [the Bible] contrary to that sense which Holy Mother Church, to whom it belongs to judge of [its] true sense and meaning, has held or does hold." During the late 1500s, the church began banning and censoring books that didn't agree with Roman Catholic doctrine.

Galileo had the misfortune to come along at a time when the church was most sensitive to change and new ideas. Even though his scientific theories challenged the way people had perceived the world for centuries, Galileo bravely continued to publish his findings. The major struggle of his life would be to try to separate religion from science. Although Galileo lost his battle against the Catholic Church, his efforts secured his place in history as the father of modern science. 🕹

# *Chapter* 2 YOUNG GALILEO

༄༅

Galileo Galilei was born in Pisa, Italy, on February 15, 1564. His mother, Giulia Ammannati, was from a noble family in Pescia. His father, Vincenzio Galilei, was a royal court musician from Florence. Vincenzio played the lute, a pear-shaped musical instrument with six pairs of strings. He would later teach his young son to play the lute, too.

Vincenzio was also a well-known songwriter. He was interested in how music and mathematics interacted. When writing new pieces, Galileo's father experimented with unusual beats and tempos. He developed theories about music that are still studied today. Vincenzio's experiments with new sounds and songs may have encouraged his son to later question, test, and experiment.

*As a student at the University of Pisa, Galileo watched a lamp swinging. He became interested in the way it moved, prompting later work with pendulums.*

Galileo was Vincenzio and Giulia's first child. In time, he was joined by two sisters and one brother. It is believed that two or three other siblings may have died in childhood, as was common in the late 1500s.

Galileo's family, although descended from nobility, was not wealthy. To please his wife, Vincenzio tried for a time to find success as a wool merchant in Pisa. In 1572, however, he gave up the textile business and moved to Florence, leaving Giulia and their 8-year-old son with relatives. Galileo's father believed that he would be able to earn a better living as a musician in Florence than as a wool seller in Pisa. At this time, Florence was considered the intellectual center of Europe.

With his father gone, Galileo studied with a private tutor. At that time, boys mostly studied Latin, as well as some arithmetic and geometry. Galileo was an inquisitive child who enjoyed exploring new ideas as well as his surroundings.

Galileo was born in a time when Italy was divided into city-states. The city-state was made up of an important city and the towns that surrounded it. Each city-state had its own rulers and government. In the late 1500s, the most important Italian city-states were the trading capitals of Venice and Tuscany. Venice, a seaport in northeastern Italy, was a wealthy shipping city. Tuscany, a collection of city-

*Galileo was born in this house in Pisa, Italy.*

states in central Italy, was controlled by the powerful Medici family. Pisa was part of Tuscany, but Florence was its most important city.

Since the 1300s, Tuscany was known throughout Europe as a center for learning, literature, and the arts. During the 14th century, the region was home to such writers and thinkers as Dante, Boccaccio,

**19**

and Petrarch. In the 15th century, the city of Florence emerged as the center of the Renaissance. Two of the most famous Renaissance figures, the artists Michelangelo and Leonardo da Vinci, came from Tuscany. In the 16th century, Tuscany—and especially Florence—continued to be a place where new ideas and theories in art, philosophy, and science were welcomed and accepted.

*Galileo received his early education at the monastery of Vallombrosa in eastern Florence.*

In 1574, Galileo and his mother joined Vincenzio in the freethinking city of Florence. Shortly after the move, Galileo traveled to Vallombrosa, a monastery in eastern Florence. Here, the young man was taught

all the things a well-educated person of the 16th century needed to know. He learned Greek and Latin. He also studied logic and religion. Galileo was very interested in religion, and he even considered becoming a monk. When Vincenzio learned of his son's wishes, he immediately pulled him out of the monastery. As the oldest Galilei son, Galileo would one day be responsible for supporting his family. He would not be able to do so as a monk.

Vincenzio decided that his oldest son would become a doctor. So in 1581, at the age of 17, Galileo entered the University of Pisa to study medicine.

Although Galileo's course of studies pleased his father, Galileo decided that medicine was not for him. Instead, he found that he preferred math and philosophy.

In Galileo's time, scholars believed that the best way to understand the world was to study the works of ancient Greek thinkers. So at the university, Galileo learned about ancient Greek theories of science and read the works of men whose ideas were accepted as fact by the entire educated world.

The ancient Greeks had developed what they felt were commonsense theories about the world around them. They tried to neatly explain the workings of Earth, sun, moon, and stars.

One of the first of the ancient Greeks to try and explain the universe was Aristotle, who lived from 384 B.C. to 322 B.C. Aristotle believed that the stars and all the other planets in the sky rotated in perfect, unchanging circles around an unmoving Earth. He also believed that the universe was perfect, unchanging, and finite. That means that he thought the universe had set boundaries. Today, we know that this is untrue. But in Aristotle's time, there were no tools to help scientists view the outer edges of our universe. Aristotle took the things he could readily observe—Earth, sun, moon, and stars—and developed a theory to explain them.

Another Greek scholar who was admired by 16th-century thinkers was Ptolemy, who lived sometime between A.D. 100 and A.D. 170 Ptolemy supported Aristotle's views of Earth as center of the universe, although he believed that the planets rotated around their own imaginary points, not around Earth. He used mathematics to develop models that could predict the motions of the planets.

Although it had been hundreds of years since Aristotle and Ptolemy had formulated their opinions

*The Greek thinker Aristotle developed theories about many scientific subjects.*

of how the world worked, learned men and women of the 16th century continued to look to the ancient Greeks for answers.

Galileo, however, was not content to just blindly accept every-thing he was taught. He argued that these Greek thinkers worked with basic ideas and observations, but not with mathematics or evidence. Galileo believed that explanations should be tested by careful experimentation. He questioned his teachers, demanding proof of the theories and ideas they presented. Before long, the quick-witted—and quick-tempered—student developed a reputation as an arguer. His teachers nicknamed him "The Wrangler."

*Theories of Claudius Ptolemy influenced scientific understanding in Galileo's time.*

In 1583, Galileo studied math with Ostilio Ricci, the court mathematician in Florence. Ricci recognized Galileo as a budding genius. He tried to convince Galileo's father to allow the young man to study math, but Vincenzio refused. Galileo defied his father and continued to focus on math and philosophy. ✑

# 3 *Chapter*

# A DEVELOPING GENIUS

೮೦೨೪

In 1585, the 21-year-old Galileo left the University of Pisa without earning his degree. He returned to Florence. Over the next four years, Galileo supported himself by giving private lessons in math and science. He also continued to study the works of the ancient Greek philosophers in his spare time. It is thought that he wrote a textbook on astronomy to use with his students.

In 1587, Galileo traveled to Rome for the first time. Here, he met the famous Catholic mathematician and astronomer, Father Christopher Clavius. Like Clavius, Galileo at this time believed that Earth was the center of the universe, with the sun and the other planets circling it.

Galileo kept his eyes open for opportunities to

*As a teacher, Galileo was popular with students but disliked by his peers.*

teach at area universities. He applied for teaching positions at the University of Siena and the University of Bologna, but he was not accepted by either school.

Despite these setbacks, Galileo's reputation as a brilliant thinker was spreading. Around 1586, Galileo invented a hydrostatic balance, a device that more accurately weighed objects in both air and water. Galileo wrote his first scientific work, a short piece called *The Little Balance*, about his invention. Possibly as a result of this discovery, the Florentine Academy asked Galileo in 1588 to give two public scientific lectures.

The following year, Galileo was given a job as a mathematician at the University of Pisa. In between lectures, he began developing and testing radical new theories of motion. His experimentation cast doubts on Aristotle's theories on falling bodies. Aristotle believed that the weight of a falling object affected its speed. According to Aristotle, if two objects of different weights were dropped from a height, the heavier object would hit the ground first. Galileo believed that the speed of two falling bodies is the same, no matter what each object weighs. He knew, however, that he needed to prove that this was true.

Galileo believed that the best way to learn about science was to experiment. Good science, he

believed, required logical thought and careful test-ing. Some of his earliest experiments were "thought experiments," tests that were carried out in his mind based on careful thought and reasoning.

*This woodcut shows the town of Pisa as it appeared in Galileo's time.*

One of Galileo's earliest thought experiments was to imagine two lead balls of different weights

Galileo also found that
as objects fall, they
accelerate, or speed up.
Nearly 100 years later,
Isaac Newton would
expand on Galileo's
work with falling bodies
to establish the laws of
gravity. Newton showed
that objects accelerate
as they fall due to
the gravitational pull
of Earth.

being tied together and then dropped. According to Aristotle's theory, one of two things should happen: Either the lighter ball will pull up the heavier weight and cause it to fall slower, or the heavier ball, when combined with the lighter one, will fall even faster.

In his thought experiment, Galileo recognized that the two would fall together. He concluded that two objects move with the same speed, no matter what their size.

Galileo also performed actual experiments to test his ideas about motion. According to Vincenzio Viviani, a later pupil and Galileo's first biographer, Galileo had his students watch as a cannonball and a smaller ball of lead were dropped from the Leaning Tower of Pisa. They were seen to fall at the same speed. Most historians doubt that Viviani's story is true. However, Galileo is known to have rolled a ball down smooth boards with varying slopes to test acceleration and speed. His experiment showed that it took less time for a ball to reach the bottom when the angle of the slope was steeper. However, the speed of the ball when it reached the end of the inclined plane always remained the same,

*Galileo performed experiments to learn about acceleration.*

no matter how steep the slope.

Throughout his life, Galileo believed that his findings on motion were some of his most important contributions to science. He wrote about his experiments in a book called *De Motu*, or *On Motion*. In the book, Galileo directly attacked Aristotle's theories. He wrote, "We certainly see by trial that if two spheres of equal size, one of which is double the other in weight, are dropped from a tower, the heavier one does not reach the ground twice as fast." Galileo, however, never published this book.

Galileo's experiments on motion upset many learned men. In 1612, one angry professor at the

University of Pisa performed his own experiments on motion. He dropped two lead balls from the Leaning Tower and found that the heavier one

*In Galileo's supposed experiment, the two lead balls landed at the same time.*

landed slightly before the lighter one. In his last books, Galileo had this to say about his opponent's test:

> Aristotle says that a hundred-pound ball falling from a height of a hundred cubits hits the ground before a one-pound ball has fallen one cubit. I say they arrive at the same time. You find, on making the test, that the larger ball beats the smaller one by two inches. Now, behind those two inches you want to hide Aristotle's ninety-nine cubits, and speaking only of my tiny error, remain silent about his enormous mistake.

*Scientists now know that air resistance affects the speed at which certain items fall. Because of air resistance, some things, like feathers, fall more slowly than other things, like rocks. This air resistance is responsible for Galileo's two balls falling at slightly different speeds. In 1969, astronaut Neil Armstrong tested Galileo's theory on the moon, where air resistance was not an issue. He dropped a hammer and a feather. Proving Galileo was correct, they reached the ground at exactly the same time.*

Galileo was popular with his students, but not as well loved by his fellow professors. The professors thought Galileo was a brash, outspoken troublemaker who was rude and abusive to those he disagreed with. To make matters worse, Galileo set himself further apart from his peers by refusing to wear the black robes worn by the other university teachers to show their rank. He even wrote a poem in which he mocked the professors and their robes.

Despite his prickly manners, Galileo had many friends and admirers. They recognized the young man's genius and encouraged him in his pursuits. Unfortunately for Galileo, most of his admirers were not employed by the university.

*This map shows Italy as it looked during Galileo's time.*

In 1591, his father Vincenzio Galilei died. As the oldest son, Galileo was now solely responsible for

taking care of his aging mother and his three surviving siblings, Virginia, Livia, and Michelangelo. This meant that Galileo had to save money for his two sisters' dowries. A dowry is money or property given to the groom's family by the bride's family upon marriage. Galileo also found himself supporting his teenage brother Michelangelo, who wanted to be a musician.

Added to the pressures at home were new pressures at the university. In 1592, Galileo's enemies began showing up at his lectures, hissing in disapproval as he spoke. When his contract at the university came up for renewal, Galileo chose not to reapply for his position. ✑

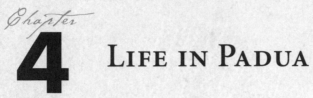

# 4 LIFE IN PADUA

 co×ɔ

Soon after he left the University of Pisa, Galileo was appointed head of the mathematics department at the University of Padua, also in Italy. The two universities could not have been more different. The university in Padua, unlike the one in Pisa, was not under the control of the Catholic Church. Instead, officials of the city-state of Venice, of which Padua was a part, made policies for the university. This allowed Galileo new freedom to pursue his unconventional ideas.

At the university, Galileo taught classes in astronomy and geometry. To earn extra money for his family, Galileo also tutored students in his home. Many of his private students were of royal birth or from wealthy merchant families. Galileo tutored these young men in mathematics, astronomy, and other subjects. But even with these added responsibilities, he still had more free time to devote to his own projects. Galileo later said that the 18 years he spent in Venice and Padua were the happiest of his life.

While in Padua, Galileo invented a number of useful devices. In 1593, for example, he invented an early thermometer. Before this time, people had no way to measure the temperature of the air around them. Galileo's thermometer, which he called a thermoscope, was very different from the thermometers of today. The device consisted of a long-necked glass bulb at the end of a glass tube. The bulb was heated, and then the entire device was placed in a container of water or other liquid.

*Although today there are many different types of thermometers that measure temperature in different ways, the most familiar kinds still operate on the same principles as Galileo's thermoscope. They measure the expansion of a liquid, solid, or gas to determine the temperature.*

As the air in the bulb cooled, liquid was drawn into the tube. The cooler the air, the more liquid entered the tube. Changes in the height of the liquid signaled changes in temperature. Galileo's simple device showed the changes in air density due to changes in air temperature. Although the instrument was not very accurate, it was one of the first measuring devices in science.

In 1597, Galileo invented an

*Galileo's thermoscope was a forerunner of our modern thermometer.*

instrument that he thought could help military commanders: the geometric and military compass. Galileo designed the compass to help armies fire their cannons more accurately. This invention was

*Galileo's geometric and military compass was a kind of early calculator.*

prompted by experiments he was performing in the field of ballistics. Having established that objects fall at the same speed regardless of weight, Galileo became interested in how objects would move if they were thrown. Once again, his work contradicted the theories of Aristotle.

Aristotle wrote that an object could only move in one direction at a time. For example, if a cannonball were shot from a cannon, it would move in the direction it was shot until its force was used up. Then the cannonball would fall to the ground. Galileo's experiments, however, showed that this was not true. Instead, when fired, a cannonball shoots forward in a smooth arc to the ground. Galileo's work in this field led to the invention of his compass.

Galileo later refined the compass so that it could be used to help solve basic mathematical problems. In 1598, Galileo invited an instrument maker to move into his home in order to build this invention. Galileo sold the compass, along with a detailed instruction manual.

During this time, Galileo was also becoming more interested in astronomy. While most people in the 16th century still believed that Earth was the center of the universe, not everyone believed that the theories of the ancient Greeks were correct. In 1543, Polish astronomer Nicolaus Copernicus had published *De Revolutionibus*, or *On the Revolutions*, which described his theory of a universe in which Earth, stars, and other planets revolve around the sun. Although Copernicus's work had not been challenged in his own time, his theory contradicted centuries of teaching, and by the late 16th century, it was viewed as a direct challenge to the Catholic Church. The book was beginning to create an uproar.

Catholics who supported Copernican theories found themselves in grave danger. Because the astronomer's theories went against the teachings of the church, those who believed them were considered heretics. Those found guilty of the crime of heresy were punished and excommunicated. Some were even killed. And yet Galileo studied the theories of the Polish astronomer, and he believed Copernicus was correct.

*In his book* De Revolutionibus, *Nicolaus Copernicus (inset) proposed the idea of a sun-centered view of the world.*

Galileo was not alone in adopting Copernicus's view of the universe. In 1597, a German scientist name Johannes Kepler published *Mysterium Cosmographicum,* or *Cosmographic Mystery,* a

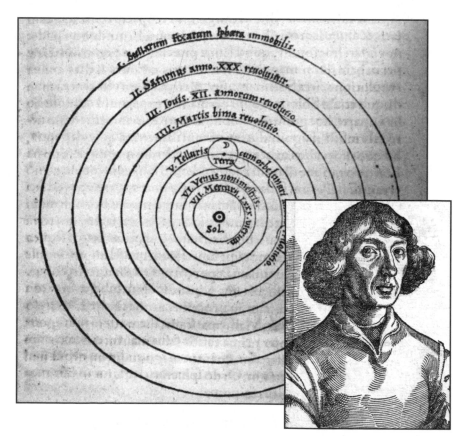

book that openly supported Copernicus's view of a universe in which all planets revolve around the sun. Galileo read Kepler's book and wrote to him later that same year, telling Kepler that he was also a Copernican. Galileo told the German that he too had used Copernican theory to explain a number of natural events. He also told Kepler that he was afraid to publish his theories, for fear of the ridicule and scorn he would suffer as a result.

*Johannes Kepler became one of Galileo's most enthusiastic supporters. In his later work, Kepler proved that the planets move around the sun in ellipses, not in circles as Galileo had believed.*

During his time in Padua, Galileo made great progress with his scientific work. His personal life, too, was going well. In the late 1590s, Galileo began a relationship with Marina Gamba, a woman from Venice. Marina was much younger and from a lower social class than Galileo. The two would never marry. However, for ten years, the two would carry on an affair that resulted in three children—daughters Virginia and Livia, born in 1600 and 1601, and son Vincenzio, born in 1606. Although Galileo could always be counted on to provide for his family, he was not an attentive partner or parent. His primary interest was his research.

In 1602, Galileo began serious experiments on the movement of pendulums. A pendulum is a hang-

*Galileo did much of his work in this tower in Padua.*

ing weight that swings back and forth. According to legend, Galileo began to develop his ideas about pendulums while a student at the University of Pisa. His interest was sparked while watching a cathedral lamp swing back and forth. Until Galileo's experiments, most scholars followed Aristotle's belief that heavy hanging objects sought to return to the center of the universe. There was no explanation in Aristotle's theories for any back and forth motion.

While performing his experiments, Galileo learned that every pendulum has its own unique period. The period is the amount of time it takes for the pendulum to swing back and forth once. Galileo experimented with altering a pendulum's period by changing its weight, length, and the arc of its swing. He found that changing the weight of the pendulum and arc of its swing did not affect the pendulum's period. The period changed only when the length of the pendulum was changed.

In the early 17th century, there were no accurate clocks. Galileo's tests allowed people to tell time more accurately. A year after his experiments, one of Galileo's friends put his discoveries to good use: Santorio Santorio, a doctor in Venice, began using a pendulum to measure the beats of his patients' pulse. ❧

# 5 A CLOSER LOOK AT THE UNIVERSE

ာ၆ာ၆၁

In 1604, a new star emerged in the sky over Italy. This was a dramatic event for the scientific community. It did not fit with the model of the universe proposed by Aristotle in the third century B.C. and believed by most people at the beginning of the 17th century. Aristotle claimed that the universe was constant and unchanging. All the stars and other planets in the sky rotated in perfect, unchanging circles around an unmoving Earth. Galileo used the appearance of the supernova to openly declare that Aristotle's theory of an unchangeable universe could not possibly be correct. He gave three lectures about the star, saying it provided proof that Aristotle was wrong.

In the spring of 1609, a friend of Galileo's told

*Galileo received support for his work on the telescope after he showed the Venetian Senate what it could do.*

him about an optical device built in Holland. Magnifying lenses had been used in eyeglasses to improve eyesight since the late 13th century. However, the Dutch spyglass was the first device used for "seeing faraway things as though nearby." It had been created as a toy.

Galileo was intrigued. He began working on his own version of the telescope. To create his telescope, Galileo first had to learn how to grind and polish glass lenses, a complicated task. In about a month, however, he had built a telescope that made objects appear three or four times larger than their normal size.

Before long, Galileo had built a telescope that could magnify objects to eight or nine times their normal size. On August 21, he traveled to Venice to show off his invention to the Senate. He asked the senators to climb to the top of a tower and peer through his telescope. The senators were astonished to see boats approaching Venice that were more than two hours away.

The display was an important professional milestone for Galileo. The senators realized the importance of Galileo's new invention to their city's safety. In exchange for the telescope, they promised Galileo a new contract that would prove too good to be true: a lifetime position as professor at the University of Padua and a pay raise that nearly doubled his salary. Unfortunately, the written contract

*These two tele-scopes once belonged to Galileo Galilei.*

was nothing like the verbal promises that were made. Not only did the contract state that he would never again get another raise, but he would also have to teach regularly until he retired. This left much less time for his research. Galileo was under-standably upset with his Venetian bosses.

In the coming months, Galileo worked to create

**47**

*Images seen through Galileo's and other early telescopes often had rainbow colors around the edges. These colors appeared because the convex lens slowed down different colors of light passing through it by different amounts. If a wave of light was slowed by the lens to a significantly shorter or longer focus than that of the image, its color would appear around the edges of the image. Most modern-day telescopes use mirrors instead of lenses. Because mirrors do not refract light, these telescopes do not show these colors.*

telescopes that were more and more powerful. In November 1609, he invented a telescope that was 15 times more powerful than the human eye. Within the next five months, he created a telescope twice as powerful as that one.

The telescope that Galileo created is known today as a refracting telescope. It was about five or six feet in length. In a refracting telescope, light enters the end of the telescope's tube and passes through a convex lens (one that is curved outward). The convex lens bends the light rays, directing them to a focal point. These light rays spread out when they hit a concave lens (one that is curved inward) at the opposite end of the tube. The rays covered more of the viewer's retina and appeared larger than normal. When Galileo looked through his telescope, the images he saw were inverted, or displayed upside down.

Galileo was the first person to use a telescope to explore the heavens. In December 1609, he began studying the moon. What he viewed further proved Aristotle's theories false. Far from being the perfectly smooth sphere Aristotle had proposed, Galileo saw with his own eyes the moon's uneven surface. He drew pictures of its mountains and craters. Every night, Galileo turned his telescope toward the moon, watching as the shadows on its face changed. He

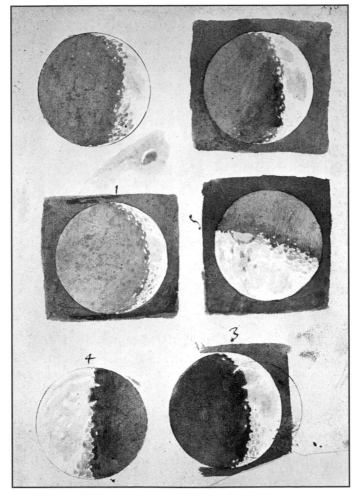

*Galileo created these sketches of the moon's phases.*

drew pictures of these changes as well, documenting the moon's phases.

In early 1610, Galileo turned his telescope toward the planet Jupiter. He wrote,

> *On the seventh day of January…at the first hour of the night, when I inspected the celestial constellations through a spyglass, Jupiter presented himself. … I saw (which earlier had not happened because of the weakness of the other instruments) that three little stars were positioned near him—small but yet very bright.*

Galileo had become the first person to observe three of Jupiter's four largest moons, also known as satellites. Days later, he discovered the fourth. Galileo named Jupiter's satellites the Medicean stars in the hope of winning favor with the Medicis, the ruling family of Florence. Today, however, they are known as the Galilean moons.

The four moons of Jupiter were the first new astronomical bodies to be identified since ancient times. As Galileo watched the four bodies over a period of months, he noticed that they never left Jupiter's orbit. Each night, Galileo charted the moons' positions, brightness, and sizes. He created 65 drawings to illustrate his findings.

With his telescope, Galileo was also the first to discover the extraordinary number of stars that

*Four largest moons of Jupiter are called Galilean moons.*

make up the Milky Way and new stars in previously known constellations. Around the nine original stars in Orion's belt and sword, for example, he identified 80 new ones. Orion's head, once thought to be made up of gases and dust, was now seen to be made up of many small stars clustered close to one another.

Although Galileo had long agreed with Copernicus's view of a sun-centered solar system, his new telescope enabled him to support this theory with observations. The more Galileo peered through his telescope at the heavens, the more convinced he became that Copernicus was correct. The longer he looked at the stars and planets, the surer he became that Earth rotated around the sun. Galileo believed that he could convince others by carefully explaining his new findings.

In March 1610, Galileo published a book called *Siderius Nuncius*, or *The Starry Messenger*, describing the discoveries he had made using his telescope. The book was an immediate hit. The first edition sold out in days, and Galileo became an overnight sensation throughout Europe. The French court even wrote to the astronomer, asking him to find a heavenly body and name it for King Henry II of France.

Not everyone was happy about Galileo's masterpiece. Many physicists who tried to verify Galileo's findings could not see any of the phenomena he described. Some refused to even look through a telescope at the skies.

Philosophers and physicists who favored Aristotle's theories called Galileo a fraud. For them, accepting Galileo's findings of an imperfect moon or a changing sky would have meant turning away from Aristotle's familiar theories. Other learned men said that Galileo had merely seen gases in the atmosphere. Although many astronomers supported Galileo's findings, still others, like Father Clavius, whom Galileo had once admired, believed that the

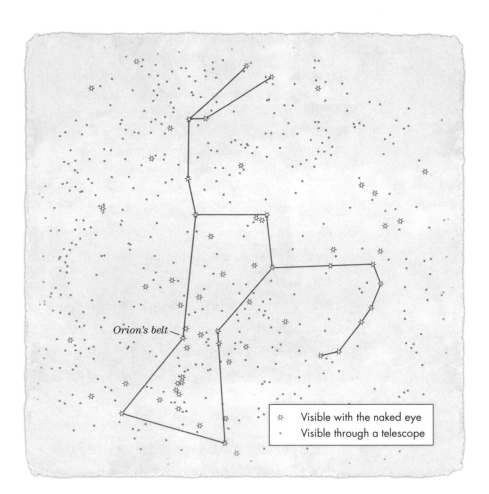

Orion's belt

| | |
|---|---|
| ✭ | Visible with the naked eye |
| · | Visible through a telescope |

findings were a result of faults in the lenses of Galileo's telescope.

To support his case, Galileo lectured in Padua. He described the experience in a letter:

*With his telescope, Galileo was able to view many new stars, such as these in the constellation Orion.*

> *The whole university turned out ... and I*
> *so convinced and satisfied everyone that*
> *in the end those very leaders who at first*

*were my sharpest critics and the most stubborn opponents of the things I had written, seeing their case to be desperate and in fact lost, stated publicly that they are not only persuaded but are ready to defend and support my teachings against any philosopher who dares to attack them.*

Most people accepted Galileo's findings as fact only after astronomers at the Collegio Romano verified them. The Collegio Romano was the scientific authority of the Catholic Church.

In the summer of 1610, Galileo was the first person to see the rings around Saturn. Galileo did not identify these new structures as rings, however. Instead, he thought that Saturn was made up of three separate parts.

Galileo was excited about his discoveries. He wanted to spend more time researching and experimenting and less time teaching. So he turned to the powerful Medici family in Florence for support. Galileo sent a letter, along with a telescope and a copy of *The Starry Messenger*, to the Medici court.

Galileo's gifts paid off. The Medici appointed him court astronomer, mathematician, and philosopher. Late in 1610, he left the University of Padua and headed back to Florence. Galileo took his two small daughters, Virginia and Livia, with him. Marina Gamba remained in Padua with their son, Vincenzio.

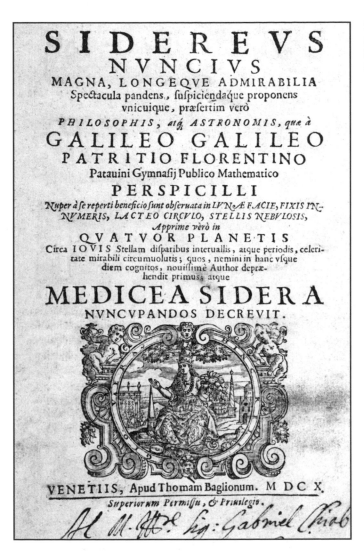

SIDEREVS
NVNCIVS
MAGNA, LONGEQVE ADMIRABILIA
Spectacula pandens, fuspiciendaque proponens
vnicuique, præfertim verò
PHILOSOPHIS, atq ASTRONOMIS, quæ à
GALILEO GALILEO
PATRITIO FLORENTINO
Patauini Gymnafij Publico Mathematico
PERSPICILLI
Nuper à se reperti beneficio sunt obseruata in LVNÆ FACIE, FIXIS IN-
NVMERIS, LACTEO CIRCVLO, STELLIS NEBVLOSIS,
Apprime verò in
QVATVOR PLANETIS
Circa IOVIS Stellam disparibus interuallis, atque periodis, celeri-
tate mirabili circumuolutis; quos, nemini in hanc vsque
diem cognitos, nouissimè Author depræ-
hendit primus; atque
MEDICEA SIDERA
NVNCVPANDOS DECREVIT.

VENETIIS, Apud Thomam Baglionum. M DC X.
Superiorum Permissu, & Priuilegio.

The Starry Messenger *became a popular success.*

In Florence, Galileo again turned his telescope to the skies. This time, his target was the planet Venus. Galileo was the first to discover that Venus, like the moon, had different phases. This proved that Venus orbited the sun, not Earth. It also proved

that Copernicus, not Aristotle, had been correct
with his theory of a sun-centered universe.

In 1611, Galileo was invited to join the presti-
gious Accademia dei Lincei, or the Academy of the
Lynxes. The academy, which was located in Rome,
is thought to be one of the first scientific societies in
the world. The founders of the academy named their
group after the lynx, a wildcat found in North
America. At this time, it was believed that lynxes
could see in the dark. Members of the academy
believed that scientists, too, could peer into the
darkness of ignorance and see what others could
not. Many of Galileo's works were later published by
the academy.

*The Accademia
dei Lincei was
represented by
this image.*

While he continued his research and experiments, Galileo also had to decide how best to care for his daughters. Because he had never married the girls' mother, Galileo knew it would be difficult and expensive to find respectable husbands for them. In 1613, he put his young daughters into the convent at San Matteo, near Florence. An admirer, Cardinal Maffeo Barberini, helped Galileo make arrangements to place the sisters there together, despite laws that prevented natural sisters from being placed in the same convent.

At San Matteo, Galileo's daughters received an education and eventually became nuns themselves. As nuns, Galileo's daughter Virginia took the name of Sister Maria Celeste, and Livia became Sister Arcangela. Over the years, Virginia would become an important source of encouragement and support for her father. ☙

S. ROBERTVS CARD. BELLARMI
E SOC. IESV.

# 6 DIFFERENCES OF OPINION

*Chapter*

❧❧❧

As a young teacher in Pisa, Galileo had antagonized his fellow professors. Over the years, he had still not learned to watch his tongue. Galileo continued to be quick to argue with those who disagreed with him. He could be sarcastic, arrogant, and unpleasant. As a result, Galileo created as many lifelong enemies as he did friends and admirers.

Back in Florence, Galileo continued to anger the learned men of the day with what they considered his wild theories. In 1612, for example, he published a book on floating bodies. In the book, Galileo defied an Aristotle supporter by stating that an object in water floats or sinks based on its density. According to the Aristotelian philosopher, an object in water floats or sinks depending on its shape.

*As a representative of the Roman Catholic Inquisition, Cardinal Robert Bellarmine demanded that Galileo stop teaching and even holding the Copernican view of the solar system.*

Supporters of Aristotle responded quickly, writing four different books to counter Galileo.

Galileo nicknamed these opponents "the pigeon league" because he thought they were a bunch of birdbrains. He disliked the way these supporters of Aristotle, when backed into a corner by facts, called upon what he termed "the terrible weapon"—the Bible. Galileo said, "… these people take refuge in Scripture, to cover up their inability to understand and to answer … arguments."

In 1612, Father Christopher Scheiner published a book about sunspots that supported Aristotle's theory that the sun is an unblemished sphere. To explain the sunspots, Scheiner proposed that they were actually small planets that revolved around the sun and blocked parts of it from view.

Galileo, too, had been studying sunspots. Since 1611, he had been looking for a way to view the sun without being blinded. First, he tried putting blue or green lenses over the end of his telescope. Next, he tried covering the lenses with soot. Finally, a student came up with the idea of projecting the sun's image onto a screen behind the telescope.

After reading Scheiner's work, Galileo wrote his own explanation of sunspots. In a series of three public letters, Galileo theorized that sunspots were probably clouds on the sun's surface. The letters ridiculed Scheiner, creating yet another enemy for

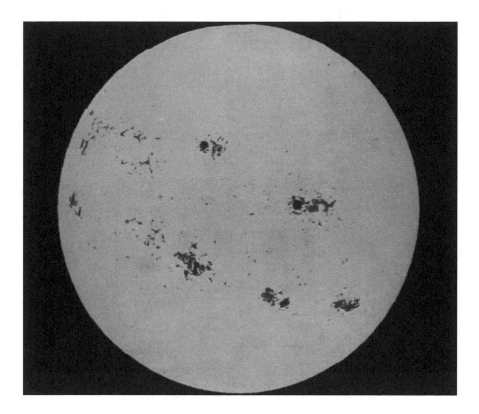

Galileo. And for the first—and only—time in his writings, Galileo directly stated his support of Copernicus's theory of a sun-centered universe.

*Galileo's work on sunspots went against Aristotle's view of a perfect, unchanging universe.*

Many priests and church officials took offense after reading the sunspot letters. In 1614, a priest in Florence, Tommaso Caccini, spoke out publicly against Galileo during a church service. Caccini also denounced any who believed that the sun was the center of the universe. He used passages from the Bible to "prove" that Galileo and his followers were wrong. Although the priest's superior wrote a letter

*In 1630, Scheiner published Rosa Ursina, in which he accepted some of Galileo's arguments and ridiculed others.*

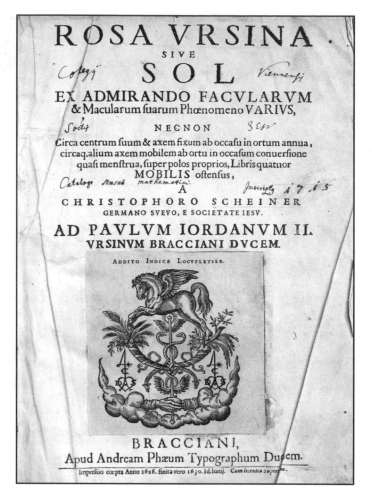

ROSA VRSINA .
SIVE
SOL
EX ADMIRANDO FACVLARVM
& Macularum fuarum Phœnomeno VARIVS,
NECNON
Circa centrum fuum & axem fixum ab occafu in ortum annua,
circaq. alium axem mobilem ab ortu in occafum conuerfione
quafi menftrua, fuper polos proprios, Libris quatuor
MOBILIS oftenfus,
A
CHRISTOPHORO SCHEINER
GERMANO SVEVO, E SOCIETATE IESV.
AD PAVLVM IORDANVM II.
VRSINVM BRACCIANI DVCEM.
ADDITO INDICE LOCVPLETISS.

BRACCIANI,
Apud Andream Phæum Typographum Ducem.
Imprefsio cœpta Anno 1626. finita vero 1630. Id.Iunij. Cum licentia superiorum.

of apology to Galileo, the scientist had his first warning of later trouble.

In February 1615, the battle between supporters of Aristotle and of Copernicus heated up. Another priest, Father Niccolo Lorini, had been given a letter written by Galileo to one of his students. In the letter, Galileo wrote that Scripture should, in arguments about science, "be reserved to the last place." Lorini sent a complaint about Galileo to the Inquisition in Rome.

The Inquisition was a branch of the Catholic Church that had been set up in 1542 to find and judge heretics. The Inquisition was especially concerned about any radical new ideas that were published in book form. In 1559, Inquisition officials started keeping a list of banned books, called the Index of Prohibited Books. All new books had to be read and approved by church censors before they could be published.

In his complaint to the Inquisition, Lorini wrote: "I have come across a letter that is passing through everybody's hands here, originating among those known as 'Galileists' ... it contains many propositions which to us seem either suspect or rash." Later in the letter, he summed up his opinion of Galileo's supporters as "men of goodwill and good Christians, but a little conceited and fixed in their opinions."

To defend himself to his supporters, Galileo wrote a new letter that addressed Lorini's complaints. The 40-page letter was addressed to the Grand Duchess Christina, the wife of Florence's ruler, Ferdinand de Medici, and the mother of Cosimo, a former student of Galileo.

In the new letter, Galileo quoted St. Augustine and other important Bible experts to show that religion and science should be separate. In the letter, Galileo argued that the Bible was written in ordinary language, rather than the language of science. The Bible was never intended to teach science. It teaches, Galileo said, "how one goes to heaven, not how heaven goes." He continued, "It seems to me that in discussing natural problems we should not begin from the authority of [Bible] passages."

No one knows for sure how many people read the letter to the grand duchess. However, a copy fell into the hands of Galileo's enemies. They sent it to Inquisition officials in Rome.

In December 1615, Galileo was summoned to Rome to defend himself and Copernicus in person. Inquisition officials read the letters Galileo had *Galileo wrote* written and found no evidence of heresy. Their *many letters about his views.* opinions of Copernicus and his theories, however,

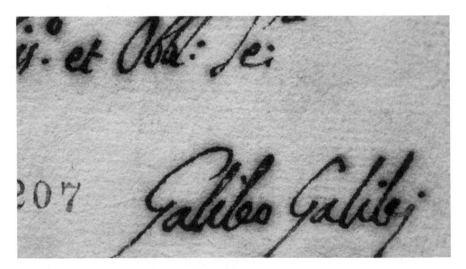

were quite different. In 1616, the Inquisition issued an internal report which stated that the idea that the sun is the center of the world was "completely foolish and absurd ... and formally heretical since it ... contradicts in many places the sense of Holy Scripture." Copernicus's book would need to be "corrected" before his theories could again be discussed.

Galileo was not yet ready to give up. A Tuscan ambassador who was with Galileo in Rome later described Galileo's drive to defend Copernicus:

> *He is passionately involved in this fight of his and does not see or sense what it involves, with the result that he will be tripped up and will get himself into trouble, together with anyone who supports his views. For he is vehement and stubborn and very worked up in this matter as it is impossible, when he is around, to escape from his hands.*

On February 26, Galileo visited Cardinal Robert Bellarmine, an important Catholic official, in Rome. Bellarmine tried to explain the Inquisition's position on Copernicus to Galileo. He also warned the scientist in no uncertain terms: Do not "hold, teach or defend [Copernicanism] in any way whatsoever, verbally or in writing." To continue defending Copernicus was, the cardinal continued, "a very

*Galileo met with Cardinal Bellarmine to discuss his works and Copernican beliefs.*

dangerous thing, likely not only to irritate all ... philosophers and theologians, but also to harm the Holy Faith by rendering Holy Scripture false."

Galileo now realized that nothing he could say or do would change the Catholic Church's position on Copernicus. His opinions were confirmed in March 1616, when the Inquisition formally "suspended" Copernicus's works until they could be "corrected." Catholic officials believed that they were protecting the authority and truthfulness of the Bible.

To protect his own reputation, Galileo asked

Cardinal Bellarmine for a letter stating that he had not been condemned by the Inquisition and clearing him of any guilt in the matter. At the end of the letter, however, the cardinal wrote that Copernicus's theories were "contrary to Holy Scripture and therefore cannot be defended or held."

After receiving his letter from Bellarmine, Galileo returned to Florence. For several years, Galileo heeded the cardinal's warnings. He stopped writing and working on supporting Copernicus's theories. Instead, he turned his attention again to motion and improvements for navigation.

Galileo's brush with the Inquisition didn't stop him from speaking his mind and attacking those he felt were foolish and ignorant, though. In 1618, three comets appeared in the skies above Italy. Their appearance defied Aristotle's theories—and the church's teachings—of an unchanging universe. Orazio Grassi, an astronomer and chief mathematician of the Collegio

*In 1616, Galileo wrote* A Discourse on the Tides. *In this paper, Galileo wrote that Earth's tides were controlled by the planet's rotations around the sun. He thought that the movement of Earth caused the planet's oceans to slosh around like water in a moving boat. He also believed that other factors affected tides, including winds, the shape and depth of the ocean, and the shape of the coastline. Today, scientists know that the gravitational pull of the moon and the sun affects the movement of the ocean's waters. Galileo's theory of tidal movement was his biggest error in a lifetime of successes.*

Romano, wrote that the comets were optical illusions and not real. Of course, Galileo couldn't let this mistake slip by, and he published his own opinions about the comets.

So began a series of written attacks exchanged between Galileo and Grassi. Galileo responded to Grassi's book with *Discourse on the Comets.* Grassi countered with *The Astronomical and Philosophical*

*Galileo's* The Assayer *was published by the scientific society Accademia dei Lincei.*

*Balance*, in which he challenged Galileo's religious beliefs. Then, in 1623, Galileo published *The Assayer*. For seven years, Galileo had resisted writing about Copernican theories, but he could hold out no longer. In *The Assayer*, Galileo again argued for a moving Earth. The book showed Galileo at his most critical. He belittled Grassi, using sarcasm and ridicule. He challenged Grassi, saying that words are not enough to prove or disprove a theory: "If [the philosophers'] opinions have the power to call into existence the things they name, then I beg them to do me the favor of naming a lot of old hardware I have about my house 'gold.'"

Once again, Galileo had made important enemies. This time, by insulting Grassi, he had also insulted the officials at the Collegio Romano. Although they had once supported Galileo, they now became angry with him. Their chance for revenge would come soon enough. ✍

# 7 GALILEO ON TRIAL

*Chapter*

芌⁓⁓

In 1623, Maffeo Barberini, an admirer of Galileo, became pope. Taking the name of Urban VIII, the new pope was more tolerant of scholars and scientists with new theories. In fact, Urban had once written a poem to honor Galileo.

In 1624, the pope invited Galileo to visit him in Rome. There, Galileo was greeted warmly. During the six weeks he stayed in Rome, Galileo met with Urban on six different occasions. He tried to convince the pope to remove the ban on Copernicus, but he was not successful. Galileo did, however, receive permission from the pope to write about Copernican theory. But the pope, who supported the theories of Aristotle, warned Galileo that Copernicus's "new astronomy" must be presented as theory, not as fact.

*In his 1633 trial, Galileo faced a courtroom of inquisitors.*

The year 1624 marked the beginning of a continuous correspondence between Galileo and his oldest daughter Virginia, now Sister Maria Celeste. Over a ten-year period, Virginia wrote dozens of letters to her father. These letters show the love, affection, and great respect the nun had for her father and his work. One letter, for example, begins, "Most Illustrious Lord Father." It ends with Virginia asking Galileo to send his newest book to her. Although many of Virginia's letters to her father still exist today, unfortunately, none of the replies from father to daughter have survived.

*Of the many letters Virginia Galilei wrote to her famous father, 124 have survived.*

In the coming years, Virginia would prove to be Galileo's chief source of comfort and support. Beginning in 1618, Galileo was stricken with bouts of poor health. Illness would trouble him for the rest of his life. Virginia constantly worried about her father's health. She offered advice and home remedies for her father to try. Soon, Virginia would stand by him during the worst period of his life.

After returning from Rome in 1624, Galileo fell ill. His sickness caused him to put off writing his defense of Copernicus's theories for a time. By 1630, however, Galileo completed the book. Before it could be published, Roman Catholic censors in Florence examined the book to make sure it did not contain anything that was against the church's teachings. The following year, they approved the book's content.

Galileo's book, *Dialogue Concerning the Two Chief World Systems*, was finally published in 1632. Galileo wrote the book in the form of a dialogue, or discussion, between three friends. The imaginary discussion takes place over four days.

The subject of the book was Copernicus's theories on the universe and how they affected the movement of the tides. One of the friends, named Salviati, favors Copernicus. Salviati is the character who speaks Galileo's views. The second friend, Simplicio, favors Aristotle. A third friend, Sagredo, is an impartial bystander. However, he is often won over by Salviati's arguments.

The characters in the *Dialogue*, although fictional, were named for people Galileo had known and admired in real life. Salviati, the Copernican, was named for a dead friend from Florence. Sagredo, the impartial bystander, was named after a dead Venetian friend. Simplicio was similar to the name of a narrator used in Aristotle's works. However, Simplicio, in Italian, also means fool or idiot.

Galileo wrote to make his arguments as easy to understand as possible. He separated the different parts of his discussion into days. On the first day, the three friends discuss motion, optics, and the characteristics of the moon. On the second day, they move on to the daily rotation of the Earth on its axis.

*Interestingly, the title page from Galileo's* Dialogue *shows Aristotle, Ptolemy, and Copernicus.*

On the third day, the three friends discuss the annual motion of the sun around Earth, or Aristotle and Ptolemy's views of the universe. In this part of the *Dialogue*, Salviati crushes Simplicio's arguments, and "proves" the rotation of Earth around the sun.

On the final day of the *Dialogue*, the three friends discuss Galileo's theory of tides. It is in this part of the discussion that Galileo makes an effort to obey Pope Urban's command and states that Copernicus's ideas are only theories, not facts. However, Galileo has the character Simplicio make this statement. Throughout the book, Simplicio has been constantly proved wrong by Salviati. Simplicio says that God can do whatever he likes and that men can never really know the truth.

When Pope Urban read Galileo's book, he felt betrayed. After all, he had supported Galileo and allowed him to write about Copernicus in the first place. Yet the pope's own views were presented by a character whose name meant "idiot." And Galileo had barely followed his order to present the new

*The dialgoue format Galileo used to discuss the various views of the solar system was already a well-established literary form in Galileo's time. In fact, Galileo's father had used the dialogue format himself in his book, Dialogue on Ancient and Modern Music. Interestingly, in his book, Vincenzio Galilei attacked Ptolemy's view of musical composition, just as Galileo attacked Ptolemy's view of the solar system in his book.*

astronomy as a theory.

To make matters worse, Pope Urban had recently been shown notes from the 1616 Inquisition banning Copernicus's writings. The notes clearly stated that Cardinal Bellarmine warned Galileo to never discuss, write about, or defend Copernicus again. Galileo's old enemy Christopher Scheiner helped convince the pope that Galileo should be punished for disobeying the Inquisition. In August 1632, publication of the *Dialogue* was halted, and Pope Urban sent orders for Galileo to come to Rome to stand trial on charges of heresy.

*In an introduction to a later edition of Galileo's Dialogue, Albert Einstein wrote that Galileo's book was "a downright roguish attempt to comply with [Cardinal Bellarmine's] order in appearance and yet in fact to disregard it."*

Galileo's friends tried to protect him from the pope's anger. They argued that the book had been approved by church censors. They pointed out that Galileo, now nearly 70 years old, was unwell. Doctors who examined the aging scientist stated that he would probably not survive the trip to Rome. An epidemic of disease in Italy at this time made traveling especially dangerous. Galileo's admirers even requested that his trial take place in Florence instead of Rome, but they were not successful. Galileo was warned that if he didn't come to Rome immediately, he would be taken there in chains.

In February 1633, Galileo arrived in Rome. Although he was not put in prison, he was ordered to stay at the home of the ambassador of Tuscany until he was called to testify. He was ordered not to socialize with others.

Galileo was to be tried for suspicion of heresy. At the time, the Inquisition defined people guilty of this crime as "those who occasionally utter propositions that offend the listeners ... those who keep, write, read, or give others to read books forbidden in the Index ... and those who listen, even once, to sermons by heretics." He was not being charged because of the contents of the *Dialogue*. Instead, Galileo was being tried for disobeying Bellarmine's 1616 warning not to defend Copernicanism in speech or in writing. The trial centered on the Roman Catholic Church's authority and Galileo's refusal to obey it. Copernicus's theories were not on trial; the Catholic Church had already banned these theories in 1616.

*Pope Urban VIII was initially a great admirer of Galileo's work.*

Galileo's trial began on April 12, 1633. Over the next two months, Galileo would be called before the Inquisition on three separate occasions. During his trial, Galileo presented the judge with the letter that Bellarmine had given him in 1616. In his own defense, the scientist stated that Bellarmine's letter showed that Copernican theories, if not presented as fact, could be "made use of." As for the first conversation, in which Bellarmine had more firmly warned him not to teach or write about Copernican theory, Galileo said he had "no memory of it, because this was many years ago."

Although Bellarmine's letter had given Galileo the proof he needed to win his freedom, the Inquisition felt he must be punished in some way. The judge met privately with Galileo, and the two made a deal: The scientist must admit to being guilty, and, in return, he would be treated with mercy.

The pope, however, was not satisfied. He insisted that Galileo be called to testify a fourth time, this time under threat of torture. Again, Galileo denied that he had written the book with any bad intentions.

On June 22, 1633, the day after his final testimony, Galileo was found to be "vehemently suspected of heresy"—just one step short of being named a heretic. Galileo agreed to publicly swear to give up his belief in Copernican theories. The elderly man, believing he would be treated fairly, said that he was

guilty of vanity and ambition. "I am more desirous of glory than is suitable," Galileo said, quoting the ancient Roman philosopher Cicero.

Galileo also signed his name to a public statement. It read,

*Copernicus's view of the sun as the center of the solar system challenged the teachings of the Catholic Church.*

> *I, Galileo, son of the late Vincenzio Galilei of Florence, seventy years of age ... abandon completely the false opinion that the sun is at the center of the world and does not move and that the earth is not the center of the world and moves ...*

After Galileo's death, a legend about this statement was born. According to the stories, after signing the document, Galileo quietly whispered, "And yet…it moves." There is, however, no proof that this happened, and historians believe that the event probably never took place.

*Galileo was forced to deny any belief in the Copernican view of the universe.*

Galileo now listened as the Inquisition listed his punishments. His statement abandoning the Copernican theory of a sun-centered universe was ordered to be read in every university. Church officials hoped to discourage others who might try to defend Copernicus and his theories. Every copy of Galileo's *Dialogue* was ordered to be burned. In addition, all Italian publishers were ordered not to print anything he wrote or even reprint anything already published. This order, however, didn't prevent publishers in other parts of the world from reprinting Galileo's works. After his trial, his books and papers were studied by scholars throughout Europe.

The final part of Galileo's punishment was especially shocking. Although the aging man had agreed to admit his guilt in exchange for mercy, he received little relief from the Inquisition. They sentenced him to imprisonment for life. ✆

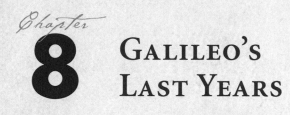

## Chapter

# 8 GALILEO'S LAST YEARS

❧❧❧

Galileo's sentence of life imprisonment was soon changed to permanent house arrest. From Rome, Galileo was sent to live with the archbishop of Siena, a man who was sympathetic to the scientist. The archbishop treated Galileo kindly and encouraged him to continue his writings on motion.

Galileo's daughter Virginia worried about her father throughout his ordeal and missed him terribly. When he was in Siena, she wrote,

> *There are two pigeons in the dovecote waiting for you to come and eat them; there are beans in the garden waiting for you to pick them. ... When you were in Rome, I said to myself: 'If he were only at Siena!' Now that you are at Siena I say:*

*Although Galileo went blind in his later years, his son helped him by writing down his ideas and drawing diagrams.*

*'If only he were at [home]!' But God's will
be done.*

After spending several months in Siena, Galileo
was allowed to return to his own villa in Arcetri,
near Florence. Galileo had purchased the country
home in 1631 in order to be closer to his daughters
at the convent of San Matteo.

*Galileo spent
the last eight
years of his life
under house
arrest in his
home in
Arcetri, near
Florence.*

Galileo was to remain in Arcetri for the rest of his life. Although he was at home, he was still a prisoner. He told his daughter that he felt as if he had been "stricken from the book of life."

In 1634, Galileo became seriously ill with a hernia. He requested permission from Roman Catholic officials to visit doctors in Florence, but the request was denied. The officials also warned Galileo if he made further requests, he would be thrown back into prison in Rome.

Galileo was soon dealt another, more serious blow. In April 1634, Virginia died. Galileo was devastated. For months, he was unable to work. In a letter to a friend, he wrote of his feelings:

> *My heartbeat is cut into with palpitations; immense sorrow and melancholy [accompany] loss of appetite; hateful to myself, I continually hear calls from my beloved daughter; ... I have at present no heart for writing, being quite beside myself so that I neglect even replying to the personal letters of friends.*

Physically ill and heartsick over Virginia's death, Galileo wrote to Catholic officials in Rome. He asked the pope to free him for medical reasons. Again, Galileo's request was refused. However, officials did agree to allow Galileo to attend church on holidays.

Galileo's blindness was a result of a cataract condition that went untreated. Cataracts formed a thin film over his eyes that slowly grew and cut off all vision. Although for years friends and admirers had asked the Catholic Church to allow Galileo to leave his home to visit a doctor, it was only after his condition became incurable that church officials allowed him to seek medical attention.

Toward the end of his life, Galileo became completely blind. For one whose career had been based on careful observation of the natural world, this was a terrible blow. Galileo wrote to a friend,

*Alas, your friend and servant Galileo has for the last month been irremediably blind, so that this heaven, this earth, this universe which I, by my remarkable discoveries and clear demonstrations had enlarged a hundred times beyond what has been believed by wise men of past ages, for me is from this time forth shrunk into so small a space as to be filled by my own sensations.*

With the help of his son, Vincenzio, and some loyal admirers, however, Galileo was able to work. He enjoyed the conversation of visitors John Milton, an English poet, and philosopher Thomas Hobbes. He also took on two assistants—a young student, Vincenzio Viviani, and the scientist Evangelista Torricelli. With their assistance, Galileo returned to his earlier studies on pendulums and timekeeping. Galileo came up with the idea of using a pendulum to make clocks work more accurately. As the aging man described his ideas, his son Vincenzio created diagrams and sketches.

Galileo's last work was *Discourses Concerning Two New Sciences*, finished in 1638. Like the book that had gotten Galileo into so much trouble,

*In his later years, Galileo worked with his son, Vincenzio, and his assistants, Viviani and Torricelli.*

*Discourses* was written in the form of a discussion. The book contains Galileo's contributions to the science of physics. In it, he refined his theories of motion and the principles of mechanics. He discussed the relationship between an object's size and its strength, the possible existence of

*Galileo's Discourses Concerning Two New Sciences was published in Holland because of the threat of the Inquisition in Italy.*

DISCORSI
E
DIMOSTRAZIONI
MATEMATICHE,
*intorno à due nuoue scienze*
Attenenti alla
MECANICA & i MOVIMENTI LOCALI,
*del Signor*
GALILEO GALILEI LINCEO,
Filosofo e Matematico primario del Serenissimo
Grand Duca di Toscana.
*Con vna Appendice del centro di grauità d'alcuni Solidi.*

IN LEIDA,
Appresso gli Elsevirii. M. D. C. XXXVIII.

atoms, the weight of air, and the speeds of light and sound. Because Galileo's works had been banned, his supporters smuggled *Discourses* out of Italy to Holland, where it was published in 1638. Many years later, Galileo's *Discourses* would inspire Isaac Newton to formulate his laws of gravity.

Galileo died at Arcetri, near Florence, on January 8, 1642. He was 77 years old. Galileo had asked that he be buried next to his father and his ancestors in the basilica of Santa Croce in Florence. However, Galileo's friends and family still feared the anger of the church. They were afraid that church officials might not allow Galileo, one who was suspected of heresy, to be buried in the church. So instead of the family crypt, Galileo was buried in a secret location in the church.

Galileo's family was right to be worried. Shortly after the scientist's death, the pope learned that the grand duke of Tuscany was planning to build a monument for Galileo. The pope sent a message to the grand duke:

> *It would not be a good example to the world ... as that man had been here before the Holy Office for a very false and erroneous opinion, which he had also impressed upon many others, there giving rise to a universal scandal against Christianity.*

Over the years, Galileo's admirers turned him into a mythic figure. He was described as a person who, in the name of science, had dared to stand up against the pope and the Catholic Church. In the

*Galileo's pupil and biographer Vincenzio Viviani funded this monument to Galileo in Santa Croce, Florence.*

GALILAEVS GALILEIVS PATRIC. FLOR.
GEOMETRIAE ASTRONOMIAE PHILOSOPHIAE MAXIMVS RESTITVTOR
NVLLI AETATIS SVAE COMPARANDVS
HIC BENE QVIESCAT
VIX. A. LXXVIII. OBIIT. A. CIƆ. IƆ. C. XXXXI.
CVRANTIBVS AETERNVM PATRIAE DECVS
X. VIRIS PATRICIIS SACRAE HVIVS AEDIS PRAEFECTIS

years following his death, Galileo's fame and legend grew. When Galileo's student and assistant Vincenzio Viviani died in 1703, he instructed in his will that his money and property be used toward the construction of a monument to Galileo.

In 1737, the monument was finally erected in Santa Croce. Galileo's remains were placed inside the monument, along with those of Vincenzio Viviani. However, those who reburied the genius kept the middle finger of his right hand as a souvenir. Today, the finger is kept in a special jar at the Institute and Museum of the History of Science in Florence. ✍

# 9  GALILEO'S LEGACY

*Chapter*

❧❀❧

**I**n the years following Galileo's death, many scientists benefited directly from Galileo's genius. They included his student Evangelista Torricelli, who created the barometer, and Bonaventura Cavalieri, who developed calculus. Galileo's work laid the foundation for Isaac Newton's pioneering work on the laws of gravity.

In addition, Galileo left behind a legacy of testing and experimenting to prove a theory. This legacy is the very basis of the scientific method that is still used today. Scientist Albert Einstein wrote, "The discovery and use of scientific reasoning by Galileo was one of the most important achievements in the history of human thought, and marks the real beginning of physics." By his example, Galileo opened up

*The telescope, triangle, magnet compass, and pendulum clock shown here all belonged to Galileo Galilei.*

a whole new approach to science.

Many argue, however, that Galileo's greatest achievement was to fight for the position of science in the world, even in the face of such obstacles as the Catholic Church.

Copernicus's view of the solar system has long been accepted by the public, but it wasn't until 1992 that the Catholic Church acknowledged its error in condemning Galileo. More than 350 years after Galileo was held in suspicion of heresy, the Catholic Church reversed its decision. In October 1992, Pope John Paul II acknowledged that church officials had made a mistake in condemning the scientist.

In recent years, there has been a surge of popular interest in Galileo. In 1999, the letters to Galileo from his daughter Virginia were collected into a book, which became an international best seller. A musical about Galileo's life opened in 2000, followed by an opera two years later.

But perhaps the tribute that Galileo would have loved best was the naming of a U.S. spacecraft after him. The 2.5-ton *Galileo Orbiter* was launched from the space shuttle *Atlantis* in 1989. Its mission was to explore the planet Jupiter. After a six-year flight to Jupiter's orbit, the *Galileo Orbiter* spent nearly eight years photographing Jupiter and its moons. It also took chemical and other measurements of the planet's atmosphere. All of this information helped sci-

*In 1989, the Galileo Orbiter explored Jupiter and its moons.*

entists on Earth learn more about Jupiter—a fitting tribute to one of science's most heroic thinkers.

The work and example of Galileo has had a lasting impression not only on the scientific community, but also on the world. Galileo's life shows the age-old conflict between science and faith, and his work emphasizing careful observation and experimentation make him one of science's most heroic thinkers. ✍

## GALILEO'S LIFE

**1579**
Sent to study at the monastery at Vallombrosa

**1564**
Born on February 15 in Pisa, Italy

**1574**
Family moves to Florence, Italy

**1580**

**1577**
Francis Drake sails around the world by way of Cape Horn.

## WORLD EVENTS

**1586**

Invents a hydrostatic
balance for weighing
items in air and water

**1581**

Attends the
University of Pisa as
a student of medicine
but instead chooses
to study philosophy
and mathematics

**1589**

Begins teaching
mathematics at the
University of Pisa

**1590**

**1588**

The English navy and
merchant ships defeat
the Spanish armada
off the coast
of France

## GALILEO'S LIFE

### 1592
Made chair of mathematics at University of Padua

### 1593
Invents the thermoscope, a device to measure air temperature

### 1597
Invents a compass to solve math problems

1595

### 1592
Japan launches an unsuccessful invasion of Korea

## WORLD EVENTS

**1609**

Creates a telescope and uses it to observe the moon's surface

**1610**

Uses the telescope to observe Jupiter, Saturn, the Milky Way, Venus, and other celestial bodies; publishes *The Starry Messenger*; returns to Florence to serve as court mathematician, philosopher, and astronomer

**1599**

Begins a relationship with Marina Gamba; the two will have three children together in the next seven years.

**1610**

**1599**

Lord Chamberlain's company builds the Globe Theatre in Southwark, London, where Shakespeare's plays are performed

**1607**

Jamestown, Virginia, the first English settlement on the North American mainland, is founded

## GALILEO'S LIFE

**1632**

*Dialogue Concerning the Two Chief World Systems* is published; summoned to Rome to face the Inquisition for defending the Copernican theory

**1616**

Writes his theory of tides; is warned by Cardinal Bellarmine to stop defending and writing about Copernicus's theory of the sun as the center of the universe

**1614**

Denounced by a priest during a church sermon

**1630**

**1614**

Pocahontas marries John Rolfe

**1620**

The *Mayflower* with its Pilgrim passengers sails from England to North America

## WORLD EVENTS

**1633**

Sentenced to life imprisonment by Pope Urban VIII

**1634**

Galileo's daughter, Sister Maria Celeste, dies at San Matteo

**1642**

Dies on January 8 in Arcetri, Italy

**1640**

**1642**

Isaac Newton, English mathematician and philosopher, is born

**1639**

The first printing press in the American colonies is set up in Cambridge, Massachusetts

**DATE OF BIRTH:** February 15, 1564

**BIRTHPLACE:** Pisa, Italy

**FATHER:** Vincenzio Galilei

**MOTHER:** Giulia Ammannati

**EDUCATION:** Attended the University of Pisa for four years

**MOTHER OF HIS CHILDREN:** Marina Gamba (About 1578-1619)

**CHILDREN:** Virginia (Sister Maria Celeste) (1600–1634)

Livia (Sister Arcangela) (1601–1659)

Vincenzio (1606–1649)

**DATE OF DEATH:** January 8, 1642

**PLACE OF BURIAL:** Santa Croce, Florence, Italy

## IN THE LIBRARY

Boerst, William J. *Galileo Galilei and the Science of Motion.* Greensboro, N.C. : Morgan Reynolds, 2004.

Hightower, Paul W. *Galileo: Astronomer and Physicist.* Springfield, N.J.: Enslow Publishers, 1997.

Hitzeroth, Deborah, and Sharon Heerboth. *Galileo Galilei.* San Diego: Lucent Books, 1992.

Sobel, Dava. *Galileo's Daughter.* New York: Penguin, 2000.

## LOOK FOR MORE SIGNATURE LIVES
### BOOKS ABOUT THIS ERA:

Christopher Columbus: *Explorer of the New World*
ISBN 0-7565-1811-8

Nicholas Copernicus: *Father of Modern Astronomy*
ISBN 0-7565-0812-6

Elizabeth I: *Queen of Tudor England*
ISBN 0-7565-0988-2

Johannes Gutenberg: *Inventor of the Printing Press*
ISBN 0-7565-0989-0

Michelangelo: *Sculptor and Painter*
ISBN 0-7565-0814-2

Francisco Pizarro: *Conqueror of the Incas*
ISBN 0-7565-0815-0

William Shakespeare: *Playwright and Poet*
ISBN 0-7565-0816-9

## ON THE WEB

For more information on Galileo, use FactHound to track down Web sites related to this book.

1. Go to *www.facthound.com*
2. Type in a search word related to this book or this book ID: 0756508134
3. Click on the *Fetch It* button.

Your trusty FactHound will fetch the best Web sites for you!

## HISTORIC SITES

Ontario Science Centre
770 Don Mills Road
Toronto, ON M3C 1T3
Canada
416/696-1000
To view copies of the handwritten books of Galileo and learn more about his discoveries

Smithsonian National Air and Space Museum
Independence Avenue at
Fourth Street Southwest
Washington, D.C. 20560
202/633-1000
To learn more about the discoveries of Galileo and other astronomers

**astronomer**
someone who studies the stars, planets, and space

**ballistics**
the study of missiles that are fired from guns

**clergy**
a group of people trained to conduct religious services

**density**
the heaviness of an object compared to its size

**doctrine**
something that is believed by a group of people

**focal point**
the point at which rays of light meet after being bent by a lens

**geometry**
the branch of mathematics that deals with lines, angles, and shapes

**heresy**
holding an opinion or doctrine contrary to church teaching

**martyr**
someone who is killed or made to suffer because of his or her beliefs

**merchant**
someone who sells goods for a profit

**optics**
a field of science that deals with light

**pendulum**
an item that hangs from a fixed point and swings freely back and forth

# Glossary

**philosophers**
people who study truth, wisdom, knowledge, and the nature of reality

**physicist**
someone who studies matter and energy

**refract**
to change direction by hitting and passing through a medium such as a lens

**supernova**
an extremely bright exploding star

**theories**
ideas or principles that explain why or how something happens

## Chapter 1

Page 12, line 2: http://www.pbs.org/wgbh/nova/galileo/science.html
Page 15, line 5: Peter Machamer. *The Cambridge Companion to Galileo.* New York: Cambridge University Press, 1998, p. 273.

## Chapter 3

Page 29, line 7: Colin A. Ronan. *Galileo.* New York: G.P. Putnam's Sons, 1974, p. 80.
Page 31, line 5: *Galileo,* p. 25.

## Chapter 5

Page 46, line 5: http://www.es.rice.edu/ES/humsoc/Galileo/Things/telescope
Page 50, line 5: Galileo Galilei. *Siderius Nuncius.* Chicago: University Press of Chicago, 1989, p. 64.
Page 53, line 5: *Galileo,* p. 44.

## Chapter 6

Page 60, line 8: Maurice A. Finocchiaro. *The Galileo Affair: A Documentary History.* Berkeley, Calif.: University of California Press, 1989, pp. 113–114.
Page 63, line 1: *Galileo,* p. 61.
Page 63, line 14: *The Galileo Affair: A Documentary History,* pp. 134–135.
Page 64, line 5: Ibid, p. 96.
Page 65, line 3: Ibid, p. 146.
Page 65, line 12: Emerson Thomas McMullen. "Galileo's Condemnation: The Real and Complex Story." *Georgia Journal of Science.* 6/22/2003.
Page 65, line 25: *The Galileo Affair: A Documentary History,* p. 147.
Page 65, line 28: *The Cambridge Companion to Galileo,* p. 282.
Page 67, line 7: *The Galileo Affair: A Documentary History,* p. 153.
Page 69, line 9: *Galileo,* p. 71.

## Chapter 7

Page 76, sidebar: http://www.pbs.org/wgbh/nova/galileo/mistake.html
Page 77, line 16: *The Galileo Affair: A Documentary History,* pp. 14–15.
Page 78, line 8: *Galileo,* p. 77.
Page 78, line 11: Ibid.
Page 79, line 1: *The Galileo Affair: A Documentary History,* p. 278.
Page 79, line 6: *The Cambridge Companion to Galileo,* pp. 23–24.

## Chapter 8

Page 83, line 10: *Galileo,* p. 79.
Page 85, line 4: Ibid, p. 80.
Page 85, line 15: Ibid, p. 79.
Page 86, line 7: Ibid, p. 85.
Page 89, line 22: *The Cambridge Companion to Galileo,* p. 418.

## Chapter 9

Page 93, line 11: http://www.pbs.org/wgbh/nova/galileo/science.html

Abbott, David, Ed. *The Biographical Dictionary of Scientists*. New York: Peter Bedrick Books, 1984.

Drake, Stillman. *Galileo*. New York: Hill and Wang, 1980.

Fantoli, Annibale. *Galileo: For Copernicanism and for the Church*. Notre Dame, Ind.: University of Notre Dame Press, 1996.

Finocchiaro, Maurice A. *The Galileo Affair: A Documentary History*. Berkeley, CA: University of California Press, 1989.

Galilei, Galileo. *Siderius Nuncius*. Chicago: University Press of Chicago, 1989.

Machamer, Peter. *The Cambridge Companion to Galileo*. New York: Cambridge University Press, 1998.

McMullen, Emerson Thomas. "Galileo's Condemnation: The Real and Complex Story." *Georgia Journal of Science*. 6/22/2003.

Reston, James, Jr. *Galileo: A Life*. New York: Harper Collins, 1994.

Ronan, Colin A. *Galileo*. New York: G. P. Putnam's Sons, 1974.

Shea, William R. and Mariano Artigas. *Galileo in Rome*. New York: Oxford University Press, 2003.

Sobel, Dava. *Galileo's Daughter: A Historical Memoir of Science, Faith and Love*. New York: Walker & Company, 1999.

Robin S. Doak has been writing for children for more than 14 years. A former editor of *Weekly Reader* and *U*S*Kids* magazine, Ms. Doak has authored fun and educational materials for kids of all ages. Some of her work includes biographies of explorers such as Henry Hudson and John Smith, as well as other titles in this series. Ms. Doak is a past winner of the Educational Press Association of America Distinguished Achievement Award. She lives with her husband and three children in central Connecticut.

## Image Credits